The endpapers of this book feature a rare and captivating moment, a group of children exploring the ocean at an exceptionally low tide. Unlike the typical images of crashing waves and full tides, this photo invites us to see another side of the sea, one that is often hidden beneath the surface.

Low tide reveals a world of wonder. A treasure trove of pools, shimmering sands and marine life waiting to be discovered. It's a time when the ocean whispers its secrets, offering an intimate glimpse into its rhythms and mysteries. For the children, it was an opportunity to fall in love with the whole of the ocean. Not just its surface beauty but its depths and intricacies, the life it cradles and the stories it tells.

This image is a reminder that every tide brings its own magic and that exploring the ocean at its quietest moments can deepen our interconnection with its boundless wonder.

First published in Far North Queensland, 2025 by Bowerbird Publishing

ISBN 978 1 7641082 1 8 (print)
ISBN 978 1 7641082 2 5 (ebook)

Our Beach
By Alison Fitzsimmons

Cover & Design: Astie Design Studio
Photography: Woven Light Co
Editing: Kellie Walsh

Distributed by Bowerbird Publishing

Available in National Library of Australia

Lightning Source

Lightning Source paper suppliers are environmentally responsible and do not use papers sourced from endangered old-growth forests, forests of exceptional conservation value, or the Amazon Basin. Lightning Source book manufacturing aims to reduce supply chain waste, greenhouse gas emissions, and conserve valuable natural resources. We share this world. We are glad to do our part in keeping it sustainable.

Bowerbird Publishing
Julatten, Queensland, Australia
www.crystalleonardi.com

A family owned Australian business

Proudly 100% Australian owned, operated & produced.

OUR BEACH

Written by Alison Fitzsimmons

Photography by Emm Wedrat

Design by Astie Design Studio

babybearschair.com.au

Australian Made with recycled paper & planet friendly inks

A Shell in a Child's Hands

The image of a small child holding a shell captures the essence of this book, a moment of curiosity, wonder and interconnection. The child's hands, so small yet so capable, represent the future stewards of our planet, cradling a piece of our Earth's story. The shell, weathered by time and tides, symbolises the deep interconnection between all living and non-living things and the ever-unfolding journey of life.

This cover is an invitation to see the world through the eyes of a child, to marvel at the simple yet profound treasures nature offers and to embrace our role in protecting it. It reminds us that even the smallest hands can carry the greatest responsibility to cherish and nurture this fragile, beautiful planet we all call home.

In those tiny hands, the past, present and future meet, a quiet but powerful message of hope, interconnectedness and the magic of nature.

An Introduction to

Our Beach

I am delighted to write this introduction to Our Beach, a luminous offering by Alison that opens pathways for children - and those who accompany them - into deeper relationship with Earth through creativity, wonder and care.

Alison understands children's innate curiosity and the importance of learning through experience. In this beautiful book, the shore becomes a classroom, the ocean a teacher, the sand and shells sacred texts. Here, children are being educated in a cathedral of life - a space unlike any other.

As Alison shares with me:

"On the morning of my granddaughter's first birthday, six one-year-old babies played in the drenching rain at Muddies on the Cairns Esplanade. A breathtaking cathedral - the mudflats, the sea, the tropical gardens, the grass, the sand, the water, the wild weather. The babies were in tight communion with one another. So too were their loving parents under umbrellas, their grandparents and great-grandparents in raincoats - and the Esplanade itself, holding us all."

This is not simply play. It is communion.

As children immerse themselves in the textures, sounds, and sights of nature, they awaken to delight, grow in creativity and discover a sense of belonging.

The photographs throughout Our Beach bring this process vividly to life. They capture moments of awe and wonder - what Brian Swimme and Mary Evelyn Tucker call "a gateway through which the universe floods in and takes up residence within us."

With care and imagination, Alison offers practical ways for parents, carers, teachers and grandparents to accompany children on this journey. Her guide invites a new generation to know, from the beginning, that Earth is alive. That breath depends on air. That water sustains life. And that the illusion of separation can fall away when we learn to see everything as connected - everything as sacred.

– Margie Abbott RSM, Cosmic Sparks

Contents

Introduction

2   Exploring the Ocean at Low Tide

7   Why The Cover Image Matters: A Shell in a Child's Hands

8   An Introduction to Our Beach

12 A Message from the Ocean

15 Why I Love Nature Play

16 The Wonder of Intergenerational Relationships

19 Getting the Most Out of This Book

20 Inspiring Wonder and Nature Play Activities

23 How Long is a Piece of String?

Inspiring nature play activities

26 The Great Wanderings Stick

29 Life Raft

30 The Lighthouse

32 Necklaces, Bracelets, Anklets, and Earrings

34 Mandalas

37 Fetch the Stick, Pearl

38 Family and Friends Totems

43 Icebergs

44 Travel Tins and Magnifying Glasses

46 Sea and White Cap Sticks

48 Sweet Dreams for Pearl: Shell Mobile

50 Mini Zen Garden

52 Sand Pies

54 Birthday Cakes

56 Mermaid, Mermen

58 Weaving

60 Lanterns and Moonbeams

63 A Tisket, A Tasket, Put Nature's Materials in a Basket

What's next?

64 Explore Numbers in Nature

67 Shapes in the Sand

68 Patterns on Shells

70 Early Literacy: Letters and Sounds

72 The Big Recount: Installations with Paper Dolls

And more

74 Be My Valentine: I Love You to the Moon and Back

77 A love Heart

78 The Christmas Star

82 Join the Mission

84 How to Become Involved as a Planet Protector

85 The Pledge

86 Taking Time to Reflect: A Moment for You

88 Taking Time to Answer: A Journey Within

89 What is Your Favourite Memory of Playing in Nature?

89 What Small Steps Can You Take to Protect our Earth Today?

90 Inspirational Quotes for Children & the Adults Who Love Them

96 In the End

98 Gratitude

100 Thank You

103 A Special Message to Claudia

104 A Word from the Author

108 Why this back cover image matters

109 About Alison Fitzsimmons

A Message from the Ocean

Hello, Little One,

I am the Ocean.
Endless.
Ancient.
Alive.

My waves tell stories and my depths hide wonders waiting for you to discover.

When you visit my beaches, feel my rhythm and hear my whispers.

I am strong but need your care.

Rubbish doesn't belong here. It hurts my creatures and dims my sparkle.

You can make a difference.

Pick it up. Protect me. Love the life I hold.

We're interconnected, you and I.

When you care for me, you care for our beautiful Earth.

With love,
The Ocean

Why I love Nature Play

There's a kind of magic in nature that nothing else can replicate. It's in the feel of sand between your toes, the sound of waves rolling onto the beach and the way sunlight dances through the leaves. It's a space where time slows down and wonder takes over.

Nature play reminds me of my own childhood. Running barefoot, collecting shells and making up stories with my sisters under the shade of a tree. It's simple, joyful and endlessly creative. Watching children today engage in these same moments fills me with hope. Their curiosity, their laughter, their natural ability to see beauty in the smallest things. This is why I love nature play.

It's not just play. It's interconnection. To each other. To our Earth. To something greater. It's a reminder that the best things in life aren't found on screens or in shops. They're right outside, waiting to be discovered.

This book is my love letter to nature and to the endless possibilities it offers for play, creativity and learning. I hope it inspires you to explore, to imagine and to cherish the world around you.

The Wonder of Intergenerational Relationships

This book weaves together the stories of children, adults and a dog, all interconnected by the ties of family and place. The children, who are all cousins, share a deep bond that extends through generations from mothers and daughters to grandmothers and grandchildren. The interconnection to the beach runs deep, as the grandmothers once played here as children, and I lived at this very beach until the age of six. The children love homemade fruit ice blocks, a simple joy that adds to their shared experiences. As for the dog, Pearl, she's a rescue pup from Cape York who proudly considers herself part beach babe, part mermaid.

Our Grandmothers Would Be So Proud!

As a child, I remember my grandmother often saying how much she adored being a grandmother. She would reflect on how busy life had been while raising her children, leaving little time to savour the moment. But as a grandmother, she embraced joy, fully present in every little moment.

Inspired by her wisdom, I hope this book helps parents and children connect meaningfully, creating moments of joy you'll all treasure forever.

Loris Malaguzzi, a visionary in early childhood philosophy, believed in the magic of discovery. He saw children as capable, curious and eager to learn through exploration. His words remind us:

"Stand aside for a while and leave room for learning; observe carefully what children do, and then, if you have understood well, perhaps teaching (or parenting) will be different from before."

Marie Montessori called young children "absorbent minds," little sponges soaking up their environment. Every interaction, every experience shapes them. That's why the best gift we can give our children is the example we set.

Be joyful. Be kind. Be resilient, creative and mindful. Show your children how to care for themselves, others and our beautiful planet.

Let Malaguzzi's words guide you:

"Nothing without joy."

Inspiring Wonder and Nature Play Activities

Designed for explorers of all ages, whether you're 3 or 103, these activities celebrate curiosity, creativity and sustainability. They invite you to mindfully beachcomb for treasures like driftwood, pebbles, feathers, leaves and shells. The key is to take only a little, leaving plenty behind for others to enjoy and for nature to thrive. Always respect the rare and protected, observing their beauty without disturbing them.

These eco-friendly, child-inspired activities encourage independent play. A responsible adult may be needed to assist with drilling small holes into shells if required. Many of the materials can be found in your craft box at home and the ideas emphasise repurposing preloved items to spark creativity while protecting the planet.

When planning a day at the beach, don't forget to bring a box for collecting rubbish. Imagine the pride on your children's faces as they leave the beach a better place, one piece of rubbish at a time. That's stewardship in action, teaching children that even small acts of care can have a big impact on the world we all share.

The true joy lies in the journey: exploring, connecting and creating while fostering a deeper appreciation for our Earth. Together, let's celebrate curiosity, joy and the beautiful interconnection that binds us to this amazing planet.

The Quintessential String Bag: Handcrafted for Adventure

Just long enough to carry the weight of a perfect day, the crochet string bags featured in this book were lovingly created by two senior women weavers with a passion for all things crochet and a deep love for nature. Eager to be part of this project to connect young children with the natural world, they created these unique bags by weaving two large circles joined with a strap perfectly sized for little adventurers.

The long strap was designed with toddlers in mind, allowing the bag to be worn comfortably across their bodies, leaving their small hands free to explore and collect treasures. The holes in the weave allow dry sand to sift out effortlessly and the bag can be dipped into the waves to wash away the wet sand, leaving treasures clean and ready to sort and use in imaginative nature play.

For drying, the strap offers a touch of practicality and charm. Hang it from a tree branch or the bullbar of your four-wheel drive, letting the treasures dry naturally in the breeze.

I love the thought that these bags might become cherished keepsakes, carried through the years. Perhaps one day, when today's small explorers have grown into adults with grandchildren of their own, they'll pull out their string bag, worn but loved, and share the tiny shells and stories of their own beach adventures.

Light, sustainable and made with care, these string bags are more than just tools - they're a symbol of intergenerational connection, the enduring magic of childhood and the shared joy of discovering the beauty of nature.

Inspiring Nature Play Activities

Wander, Wonder and Create

Every adventure leaves behind a story and your Great Wanderings Stick is the perfect way to hold onto those memories. As you explore, let nature inspire you, but remember, we're here to celebrate and protect it. Collect only a little, taking just enough to spark your creativity while leaving plenty behind for others and for nature to thrive. For this activity, we'll use jute string. It's a sustainable, natural material that's kind to our Earth and perfect for this project.

You'll Need to Collect:

- A long, straight piece of driftwood
- Small treasures from nature: shells, feathers, leaves, or seaweed (*Tip: Take only a little and never what's rare or protected. Love our Earth as you would family. Leaving it as beautiful as you found it and honour the interconnection we all share.*)
- A long piece of sustainable string such as jute twine or bamboo cord.

Now Create:

- Use the jute string to attach your treasures to your driftwood stick.
- Store your Great Wandering Stick somewhere special, where you can see it and remember your adventures.
- Keep wandering and wondering - each journey you can add a new treasure to your stick.
- Share your wandering stories with friends and family and let your stick inspire others to explore and protect nature.

Your Great Wandering Stick is more than an activity, it's a tribute to the wonders of our Earth and a reminder of the adventures that await.

Life Raft

Create a Raft of Memories

The Life Raft is more than an activity; it's a way to capture the spirit of the sea and the stories carried by the tides. As you gather materials, remember to tread gently. Take only a little and leave behind treasures for others to discover. Let's honour and protect the natural world as we create.

For this project, we'll use sustainable string, like jute twine or bamboo cord, to tie our raft together. These materials are kind to our Earth.

You'll Need to Collect:

- 7 or 8 small pieces of driftwood, snugly fitting together *(**Tip:** Take only a little and never what's rare or protected. Love our Earth as you would family. Leaving it as beautiful as you found it and honour the interconnection we all share.)*

- A long piece of sustainable string such as jute twine or bamboo cord

Now Create:

- Arrange the driftwood sticks in a way that feels just right to you.

- With the help of an adult, tie a knot onto the first stick.

- Wrap the string three times around each stick, gently pulling to keep the pieces snugly together.

Display Your Life Raft:

Turn your creation into a lasting memory:

- Repurpose an old shadow box.
- Place the Life Raft inside and display it as a piece of art.
- Add a handwritten note or drawing to tell the story of where and how you found the materials.

Your Life Raft is a small reminder of the sea's beauty and power. Each stick holds a story and together, they become a tribute to the ocean's endless wonders.

A Beacon of Creativity and Connection

Inspired by the iconic lighthouse, this activity is a way to bring the magic of sunrises, sunsets and moonlit nights into your home. Just like the lighthouse guides ships to safety, let this project remind you of the importance of protecting and respecting our natural world.

As you gather materials, take only a little and always leave the environment as beautiful as you found it. This lighthouse is not just art, it's a symbol of care and interconnection.

You'll Need to Collect:

- A straight, rounded piece of driftwood (**Tip:** *Take only a little and never what's rare or protected. Love our Earth as you would family. Leaving it as beautiful as you found it and honour the interconnection we all share.*)
- White non-toxic paint (in squeeze tubes is easiest to apply)
- Red non-toxic paint
- A small soft sponge like a piece of a kitchen sponge
- A black sharpie

Now Create:

- Lay your driftwood down and squirt some white paint onto it.
- Use the sponge to coat the stick in white paint, turning it to cover all sides and ends.
- Let the white paint dry completely, turning the stick occasionally to ensure an even finish.
- Once dry, dab red paint onto the edge of the sponge and carefully add red stripes, alternating between white and red. End with red at the top to represent the lighthouse roof.
- Allow the paint to dry thoroughly.
- With the black sharpie, draw small windows within the red stripes and a door at the base of the stick to complete your lighthouse.

Your Lighthouse, Your Story:

Display your lighthouse where it can inspire you and others. Perhaps near a window or on a shelf with other natural treasures. Let it serve as a reminder of the beauty of the sea and the simple joys of creating with care for the planet.

This Lighthouse isn't just a craft, it's your beacon of creativity, sustainability and interconnection to the world around you.

Necklace, Bracelet, Anklet and Earrings

Wear the Ocean's Beauty

Celebrate the simplicity and charm of nature by creating jewellery inspired by the treasures of the sea. Every shell you collect holds a memory of your time by the water. As always be mindful, take only a little, leaving plenty behind for others to discover and for nature to thrive. For this activity, we'll use sustainable string, like jute twine or bamboo cord, honouring our commitment to care for our Earth.

You'll Need to Collect:

- Shells with natural holes *(Tip: Take only a little and never what's rare or protected. Love our Earth as you would family. Leaving it as beautiful as you found it and honour the interconnection we all share.)*

- A long piece of sustainable string such as jute twine or bamboo cord.

Now Create:

- Necklace
  - Thread the shells onto a long piece of string.
  - After adding each, you can tie a small knot to keep it in place.
  - Once all your shells are threaded, tie the ends of the string together to complete your necklace.
- Bracelet and Anklet:
  - Use a shorter piece of string and thread shells onto it.
  - Tie the ends together to create a bracelet or anklet that fits snugly around your wrist or ankle.
- Earrings:
  - Thread a small shell onto an earring base, such as a sleeper or small hoop.
  - Secure the shell in place, creating a simple yet beautiful piece of wearable art.

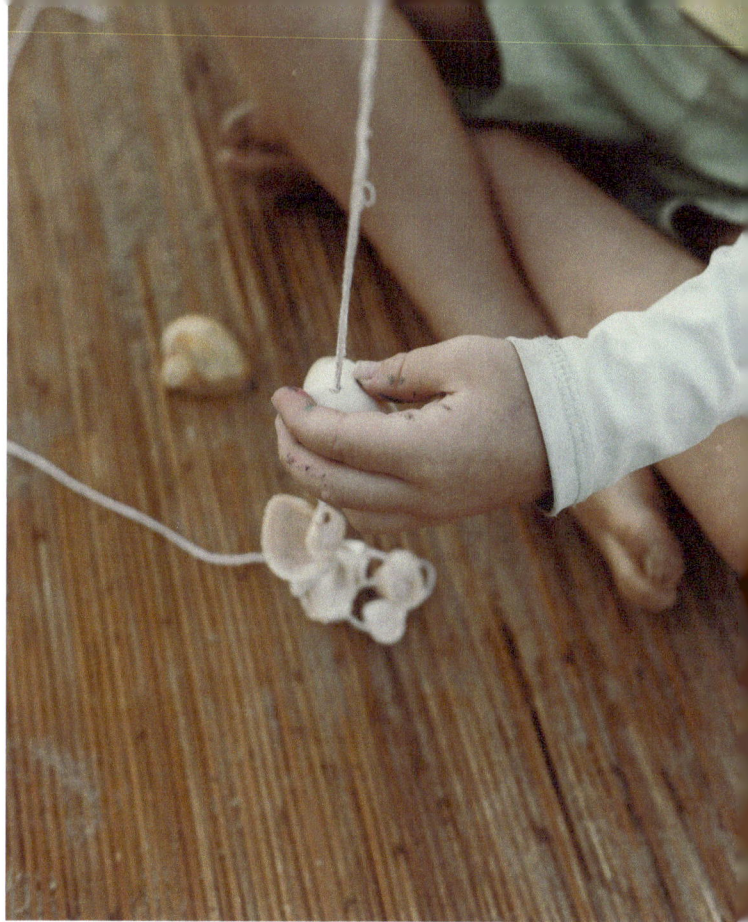

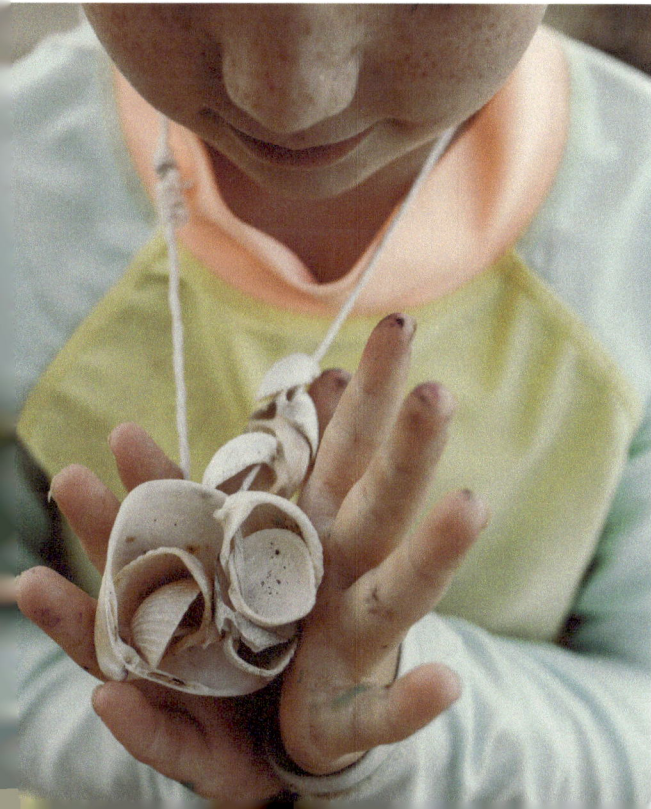

Your Jewellery, Your Story:

Each piece of jewellery you create is more than an accessory. It's a connection to the ocean and a reflection of your respect for the natural world. Wear your creations proudly and let them remind you to wander with wonder and tread lightly wherever you go.

Whether it's a necklace, bracelet, anklet or pair of earrings, your ocean-inspired jewellery carries the story of your love for our Earth.

Mandalas

Create Patterns That Honour Nature

Mandalas are more than just art; they are a celebration of symmetry, balance and the beauty of the natural world. Inspired by the intricate patterns of Turkish tiles, these creations are a way to express gratitude for the treasures our Earth offers.

As you gather items for your mandala, remember to tread gently. Take only what you need, leaving plenty behind for others to enjoy and for nature to flourish.

You'll Need to Collect:

🌊 Small collections of shells, seeds, pods and stones in various colours and sizes *(Tip: Take only a little and never what's rare or protected. Love our Earth as you would family. Leaving it as beautiful as you found it and honour the interconnection we all share.)*

Now Create:

🌊 Choose a flat surface to work on. This could be sand, soil or a large piece of paper.

🌊 Start in the center of your mandala with one item, such as a shell or stone.

🌊 Gradually build outward in concentric circles, arranging your treasures carefully.

🌊 Alternate colours, shapes and textures to create stunning patterns that reflect the harmony of nature.

🌊 Step back often to admire your work and adjust as needed to maintain balance.

Your Mandala, Your Moment:

Once complete, your mandala can be left as a gift for nature, returned to Earth where it belongs, or photographed as a keepsake. If indoors, display it as a centerpiece to share its beauty with others.

Creating mandalas is an act of mindfulness and gratitude. Each pattern tells a story of your interconnection to our Earth and your commitment to its care.

A Playful Bond with Nature

This activity is perfect for creating a special toy for your four-legged friend while celebrating the beauty of natural materials. Inspired by the joy of play, it combines creativity with sustainability. As always be mindful. Take only what you need and leave plenty behind for others to discover and enjoy.

You'll Need to Collect:

- A stick that feels sturdy and fits comfortably in your hand *(**Tip:** Make sure it's safe for throwing and free of sharp edges or splinters.)*

- A long piece of sustainable string such as jute twine or bamboo cord.

- Small shells with natural holes

Now Create:

- Select a stick that feels just right for throwing. Practice a few gentle tosses to ensure it's suitable for your dog to retrieve.

- Gather small shells with natural holes or a responsible adult may be needed to assist with drilling small holes into shells if required.

- Bind the shells securely to one end of the stick using a sustainable string. Wrap tightly so they stay in place during play.

Play and Connect:

Head to the beach, park or backyard and let the fun begin! Toss the stick for your dog and enjoy the simple joy of shared playtime.

Your Fetch the Stick, Pearl creation is more than just a toy. It's a way to connect with your pet, appreciate the natural world and tread lightly on the planet.

A Driftwood Tribute to Your Tribe

Celebrate the people you love with this creative and meaningful project. Using simple materials from nature, you'll create a unique "family portrait" that honours your connections while reflecting the beauty of the natural world. As always, gather with care. Take only what you need and leave the rest for others to enjoy.

You'll Need to Collect:

- Several pieces of driftwood in different lengths *(**Tip:** Let each piece represent a different family member or friend whether tall, small or somewhere in between. Take only a little and never what's rare or protected. Love our Earth as you would family. Leaving it as beautiful as you found it and honour the interconnection we all share.)*

- A black sharpie

- A bowl of beach sand

Now Create:

- Look at each piece of driftwood and imagine which family member or friend it might represent.

- Using the black sharpie, draw a simple face on each piece. Keep it playful and fun!

- Fill a bowl with beach sand and stand the driftwood pieces upright in the sand, arranging them like a group family photo.

Your Totems, Your Story:

Display your Family and Friends Totems in a special spot where they'll remind you of the people you cherish. Each piece of driftwood carries its own story, shaped by the waves and winds, just like the lives of those it represents.

This activity is more than art. It's a celebration of family, friendship and the interconnectedness of all things.

Icebergs

Discover Frozen Wonders

Explore the magic of nature and science with this exciting, planet-friendly activity. Your Iceberg becomes a frozen treasure chest filled with sea creatures and natural wonders. By creating it in layers, you'll uncover surprises as you go, celebrating sustainability while having fun.

You'll Need to Collect:

- A large, freezer-safe bowl

- Small, plastic sea creatures or treasures like shells, twigs, pods, grasses or leaves (*Tip: Take only a little and never what's rare or protected. Love our Earth as you would family. Leaving it as beautiful as you found it and honour the interconnection we all share.*)

- Scouring tools such as a fork, spoon or old toothbrush

Now Create:

- Place a layer of collected treasures at the bottom of the bowl.

- Add enough water to cover the first layer, then place the bowl in the freezer until solid.

- Once frozen, add another layer of treasures and water. Repeat the process, freezing layer by layer, until the bowl is full.

- When all the layers are frozen, remove the iceberg from the bowl.

The Big Excavation:

- Set your iceberg on the sand, in a tray or shallow tub.

- Use your scouring tools to carefully excavate each layer, revealing the treasures hidden within.

- Observe how the ice melts and exposes each item, marvelling at the patterns and textures.

Your Iceberg Adventure:

This activity blends creativity, exploration and sustainability. Each layer of your iceberg tells a story of nature's beauty while demonstrating the importance of mindful choices. The choosing of reusable bowls over balloons because celebrations need not come at the cost of our Earth, and joy is even brighter when it leaves no waste behind. Your Iceberg is a testament to the wonder of discovery and the joy of protecting our planet.

A Tiny World of Wonder

Dive into creativity by crafting a tiny world that captures the magic of nature and cherished memories. This activity invites you to use natural materials and repurposed items to create a little world of your own. These tiny worlds inside travel tins are perfect companions, small enough to carry with you wherever you go, keeping a piece of nature close at hand. As always, tread lightly and collect only what you need, leaving plenty for nature to thrive.

You'll Need to Collect:

- Tiny shells (*Tip: Take only a little and never what's rare or protected. Love our Earth as you would family. Leaving it as beautiful as you found it and honour the interconnection we all share.)*

- Sand

- Drawings of your child and/or pet, ensuring the images are small and clear

- Repurpose a small, preloved keepsake box with a tight-fitting lid to create a travel tin, perfect for storing treasures or memories from your adventures

Now Create:

- Sprinkle sand across the base of the box to form a miniature beach.

- Cut the drawings into small rectangular shapes to make free-standing paper dolls.

- Position the paper dolls in the scene, arranging them to interact with the "beach" and "shells."

- Adjust and add any finishing touches until the scene feels just right.

Explore and Share:

Display your tiny world where it can spark curiosity and wonder. Pair it with a magnifying glass to encourage close inspection, inviting friends and family to appreciate the tiny details. Carry your travel tin with you to preserve a piece of nature and spark storytelling wherever you go.

This activity isn't just about creating a scene. It's about telling a story, celebrating the beauty of nature and creating a keepsake that connects loved ones to the natural world.

Sea and White Cap Sticks

Bring the Ocean Home

This activity is inspired by the gentle rhythm of waves and the peaceful colours of the sea. Your Sea and White Caps are a simple yet beautiful way to capture the essence of the ocean. As always, collect with care, choosing only what you need and leaving the beach as beautiful as you found it.

You'll Need to Collect:

- Driftwood in various lengths *(**Tip:** Let the shapes and sizes remind you of the waves breaking on the shore. Take only a little and never what's rare or protected. Love our Earth as you would family. Leaving it as beautiful as you found it and honour the interconnection we all share..)*

- Non-toxic acrylic white paint in a tube

- Non-toxic acrylic blue paint in a tube

- A small sponge

- A bamboo bowl filled with beach sand

Now Create:

- Use the sponge to cover each driftwood stick with white paint, giving it the look of frothy sea caps.

- Allow the paint to dry completely.

- Once dry, use the sponge to add a band of blue paint around the stick, evoking the deep hues of the ocean.

- Let the paint dry thoroughly.

Display Your Sea Sticks:

- Arrange the painted driftwood sticks in a bamboo bowl filled with beach sand.

- Add finishing touches to bring your scene to life. Perhaps a few small boats nestled among the sticks or shells scattered at the base. To complete the experience, play soothing ocean sounds on Spotify and let your display transport you to the gentle rhythm of the sea.

Your Ocean-Inspired Display:

This simple yet elegant craft brings the tranquility of the sea into your home It's more than decoration - it's a connection to the natural world and a gentle reminder of the ocean's beauty and power. Your Sea and White Caps will fill any space with the calming energy of the waves, inspiring you to protect and cherish the sea every day.

A Soothing Symphony of the Sea

Creating a shell mobile is a beautiful way to bring the calming sounds and sights of the ocean into your space. As you create, remember to tread lightly, taking only what you need and leaving rare or fragile shells for nature to cherish.

You'll Need to Collect:

- A straight piece of driftwood
- Shells with natural holes (**Tip:** *Take only a little and never what's rare or protected. Love our Earth as you would family. Leaving it as beautiful as you found it and honour the interconnection we all share.*)
- A long piece of sustainable string such as jute twine or bamboo cord.
- Scissors

Now Create:

- Rinse your collected shells with seawater and let them dry in the sun. This enhances their natural beauty.
- Cut five lengths of string, varying in lengths to create a cascading effect for the mobile.
- Start with one string and tie a double knot near the bottom. This knot will hold your bottom shell in place.
- Thread the string through the first shell and tie another knot about 3 cm above it. Continue this process until you've added all the shells.
- Repeat the steps for the remaining four strings.
- Attach each string of shells to the driftwood, spacing them evenly along its length.
- Finally, tie a piece of string to both ends of the driftwood, creating a loop for hanging your mobile.

Display Your Mobile:

Hang your Sweet Dreams for Pearl Shell Mobile above your pet's bed. As she drifts off to sleep, imagine Pearl - our beloved dog who proudly believes she's part beach babe and part mermaid - being lulled by the soft clinking sounds and gentle sway of the shells. In her dreams, she'll chase sticks and swim joyfully with her family at the beach. Place the mobile where it can catch a breeze, like near a window or on a verandah, adding a touch of ocean magic to her cozy space - and to yours.

Your Ocean-Inspired Keepsake:

This mobile is more than a decoration; it's a lullaby of the sea, a reminder of peaceful beach days and a call to protect the natural world. Let it inspire sweet dreams and a deep connection to the ocean.

Find Calm in Every Grain of Sand

Creating a Mini Zen Garden is a mindful way to bring the tranquility of nature into your daily life. The gentle act of raking patterns in the sand and arranging stones encourages relaxation, focus and creativity. As aways, collect mindfully. Take only what you need and leave the rest for nature to flourish.

You'll Need to Collect:

- Tools for creating patterns: mini rakes, back scratchers, skewers, toothpicks or forks
- A container that reflects your personal style *(Tip: A shallow wooden box or ceramic dish works beautifully.)*
- Sand (fine grain sand shows patterns best)
- Small stones *(Tip: Take only a little and never what's rare or protected. Love our Earth as you would family. Leaving it as beautiful as you found it and honour the interconnection we all share.)*

Now Create:

- Fill your container with sand, smoothing it out to create an even surface.
- Choose stones to place in your garden. These are the heart of your Mini Zen Garden, so arrange and rearrange them as often as you like.
- Use your mini rake or tools to create patterns in the sand around the stones. Try wavy lines, concentric circles or anything that feels calming.

Tend Your Garden Daily:

- Your Mini Zen Garden is more than an activity. It's a practice of mindfulness.. Each time you rake the sand or rearrange the stones, you bring a sense of calm and creativity into your day.

Your Zen Space, Your Story:

Place your Mini Zen Garden where you can see and use it often. Let it remind you to pause, breathe and connect with the simple beauty of nature.

From Mud to Sand:
The Joy of Seaside Kitchens

Who can resist the timeless fun of creating pies from nature? This activity takes the beloved mud kitchen to the beach, turning sand, water and natural treasures into playful masterpieces. As always, collect mindfully, taking only what you need and leaving plenty behind for others and for nature.

You'll Need to Collect:

- Natural items like rocks, shells, leaves, and grass (*Tip: Look for materials already scattered about rather than picking fresh ones. Take only a little and never what's rare or protected. Love our Earth as you would your own family. Leave her as beautiful as you found her, honouring the interconnection we all share.*)

- Preloved candles or small sticks to represent candles

- A mixing spoon or sturdy stick

- An old towel or rag for cleanup

- Preloved containers, bottles and ladles for holding and carrying seawater

- Preloved bowls, pots, pans, muffin tins and cake tins. Repurposing kitchen items adds to the fun and sustainability!

Now Create:

- ~ Scoop some sand into a bowl and gradually mix in seawater with a spoon or stick.

- ~ Stir well until you reach the perfect "pie dough" consistency. Firm enough to shape but still wet.

- ~ Use spoons to scoop the wet sand into old pots, pans or muffin tins, shaping your sand pies.

- ~ Decorate the tops with shells, stones, leaves and preloved candles or use small sticks as "candles" to create celebratory pies.

- ~ Experiment with textures and designs. Each pie is a unique creation!

Extend the Play:

Once your sand pies are "baked" in the sun, pretend to serve them up or start fresh with new designs. Wash and wipe your tools when finished to keep them clean and ready for the next adventure.

Your Sand Kitchen, Your Creation:

Whether it's a simple pie or an elaborate "cake," every creation tells a story of imagination, interconnection and respect for nature. Let your seaside sand kitchen inspire hours of joy and creativity, leaving nothing behind but happy memories.

Celebrate by the Sea

Who can resist the fun of creating beach birthday cakes? This activity takes the joy of mud cakes to the beach, combining nature play with creativity. With a little sand, water and imagination, every day can feel like a celebration. As always, collect thoughtfully, taking only what you need and leaving the beach as you found it.

You'll Need to Collect:

- ∿ Natural items like rocks, shells, leaves, and grass (*Tip: Look for treasures already scattered along the shore. Take only a little and never what's rare or protected. Love our Earth as you would your own family. Leave her as beautiful as you found her, honouring the interconnection we all share.*)

- ∿ A mixing spoon or sturdy stick

- ∿ Containers, bowls, bottles and ladles for carrying seawater

- ∿ Reuse old birthday candles

- ∿ A preloved springform round cake pan or ice-cream bucket with the base cut out to create a bottomless bucket

Now Create:

- ⌇ Start by finding a good spot to build your sand birthday cake.

- ⌇ Alternate layers of sand and water inside the springform cake ring or bottomless bucket: add sand, pour water, and repeat. This creates the perfect consistency to hold its shape.

- ⌇ Using your mixing spoon or stick to pack the sand firmly into your springform cake ring or bottomless bucket as you go.

- ⌇ Once full, pat the sides of your springform cake ring or bottomless bucket gently to loosen the sand.

- ⌇ Carefully lift the springform cake ring or the bucket off to reveal a sturdy cake base.

- ⌇ Decorate your cake with shells, stones and other treasures. Add candles to complete your masterpiece.

Make It Magical:

Take photos of your sand birthday cakes or enjoy an imaginary beach celebration with friends and family. Then, when the fun is over, leave the decorations behind for nature or collect them to reuse another time.

A Legendary Connection to the Sea:

Every birthday cake is a reminder of how simple things like sand, water and natural treasures can spark endless creativity and joy.

Mermaid, Merman

Transform into a Sea Legend

Bring the magic of the ocean to life by creating a mermaid or merman in the sand! This playful activity is perfect for sparking imagination and connecting with nature. As always, collect shells mindfully, taking only what you need and leaving the beach as beautiful as you found it.

You'll Need to Collect:

- Buckets and spades
- Preloved old spoons and forks
- Shells (*Tip:* *Take only a little and never what's rare or protected. Love our Earth as you would your own family. Leave her as beautiful as you found her, honouring the interconnection we all share.*)

Now Create:

- Pick Your Spot: Find a shaded area to work in, as this activity takes time and creativity.
- Outline the Shape: Have the child sit on the beach, and use a stick to outline a mermaid or merman tail around their legs.
- Dig the Base: Once the outline is complete, the child can step out while you dig out some sand to create a sunken base.
- Form the Shape: The child sits in the sunken base and together you begin piling sand around them. Use buckets of sand to sculpt the mermaid or merman shape.
- Add the Details: Use a stick or old fork to draw scales on the tail. Decorate with shells to complete the transformation.

Make It Magical:

Encourage storytelling as you work. What kind of mermaid or merman are they? What treasures do they protect in the ocean? Once finished, take a photo to remember your sandy creation before it's reclaimed by the tide.

A Legendary Connection to the Sea:

This activity is more than just fun; it's a chance to spark imagination, celebrate creativity and deepen your connection to the natural world. Let the magic of your Mermaid or Merman bring joy to the beach and memories that last long after the sand has washed away.

Weaving

Nature's Loom of Creativity

Weaving with natural materials is a beautiful way to connect with the environment while creating something unique and mindful. This craft invites you to explore textures, patterns and colours in nature while respecting the world around you. As always, collect thoughtfully. Take only what you need and leave plenty for others to enjoy and for nature to thrive.

You'll Need to Collect:

- 4 sticks of driftwood, roughly the same length *(Tip: Choose sturdy pieces to form your loom.)*

- A long piece of sustainable string such as jute twine or bamboo cord

- Leaves, small branches, shells, and pods *(Tip: Take only a little and never what's rare or protected. Love our Earth as you would your own family. Leave her as beautiful as you found her, honouring the interconnection we all share.)*

Now Create:

Step 1: Build the Loom

- Overlap the driftwood sticks to form a rectangle.

- Have an adult bind the corners securely with sustainable string, ensuring the loom is sturdy.

Step 2: Add the Warp

- Tie the string to the bottom-left corner of the loom.

- Use a figure-8 motion to wind the string over the top stick and back down to the bottom stick.

- Continue this process across the loom until it is evenly strung, creating the warp.

- Tie off the string at the bottom-right corner to secure it.

Step 3: Weave Your Materials

- Begin weaving your natural treasures - leaves, grasses, shells, and pods - through the warp strings.

- Alternate over and under as you weave, creating patterns and textures.

- Adjust your materials as needed to balance the colours and shapes.

Your Woven Creation:

Once complete, display your loom in a special spot, such as a window or outdoor space, where it can remind you of your connection to nature.

A Loom of Mindfulness and Respect:

This weaving activity is more than a craft - it's a mindful exploration of nature and creativity. Let each thread and treasure tell a story of care, interconnection and the beauty of the natural world.

Lanterns and Moonbeams

Light Up the Night with Nature's Touch

Create a magical glow for your evenings with this simple and sustainable lantern. Using recycled materials and natural elements, this craft brings together creativity, care for the planet and the beauty of a soft, warm light.

You'll Need to Collect:

- A recycled paper shopping bag with a flat base and handles (*Tip:* *White bags work best for a moonbeam effect.*)

- A long, straight piece of driftwood (*Tip:* Choose thoughtfully, leaving enough driftwood behind for nature. Take only a little and never what's rare or *protected*. Love our Earth as you would your own family. Leave her as beautiful as you found her, honouring the interconnection we all share.)

- A sharp small stick.

- A long piece of sustainable string such as jute twine or bamboo cord.

- A battery-operated tealight.

Now Create:

Step 1: Prepare the Paper Bag

∿ Carefully pierce small holes in each side of the paper bag using the sharp stick. These holes will allow the light to shine through, creating beautiful patterns.

Step 2: Add the Light

∿ Place the battery-operated tealight inside the bag.

Step 3: Assemble the Lantern

∿ Tie the handles of the bag securely to the driftwood stick using the sustainable string. Ensure the string is strong and well-secured.

Display Your Lantern:

Hold your Lantern and Moonbeams as you take an evening stroll, or hang it in a special spot to light up your surroundings with its soft glow.

A Glow of Wonder:

Your lantern is more than just light. It is a reminder of how recycled and natural materials can come together to create something magical. Let it inspire quiet moments of reflection and a deep connection to the beauty of the world around you.

Getting Even More Out of Your Natural Materials

Storing your collected treasures in a basket isn't just practical. It's a way to honour the tradition of handmade, eco-friendly craftmanship. Women around the world have woven baskets from natural materials for generations, creating both beauty and utility.

Why Choose Handmade Baskets?

- Handmade baskets crafted from materials like jute, bamboo or grasses are sustainable and biodegradable.
- By opting for these over plastic, you're helping to reduce waste and protect the planet.
- Each basket has its own story, connecting you to the skilled hands that made it and the tradition it represents.

Where to Find Them:

- Local markets often sell unique, handmade baskets made from natural materials.
- Secondhand and thrift stores are great places to discover preloved treasures, giving them a second life.

Say No to Plastics:

Every time you choose natural alternatives, you're making a small but powerful statement to care for our Earth. A simple basket filled with your collected leaves, shells and driftwood becomes more than storage. It's a symbol of sustainability and respect.

Embrace the Tradition:

Let your basket be a reminder of the beauty of craftsmanship and the importance of living lightly on the planet. Fill it with natural materials, use it for beachcombing or keep it as a special place to hold your treasures.

Choose wisely, tread lightly, and celebrate the stories woven into every strand.

Early Numeracy: My Favourite Number is 3

Engaging with early numeracy through natural materials combines learning and creativity in the most delightful way. By crafting your favourite numbers using shells, leaves, or stones, children not only explore maths but also connect with the beauty of the natural world. As always, collect thoughtfully and leave plenty for nature to thrive.

You'll Need to Collect:

- Shells, leaves, and stones (*Tip: Take only a little and never what's rare or protected. Love our Earth as you would your own family. Leave her as beautiful as you found her, honouring the interconnection we all share.)*

Now Create:

- Choose your favourite number. Why not start with 3?
- Trace Your Numbers: Use a stick to trace the number in the sand or dirt before placing your materials.

Extend the Play:

- Count as You Create: Practice counting the materials as you place them to reinforce early numeracy skills.
- Carefully arrange your collected materials on a flat surface and write the number.
- Compare and Explore: Create other numbers and compare amounts.

A Simple Lesson with Big Impact:

- This activity makes early numeracy fun, tactile and connected to the environment. Let My Favourite Number is 3 inspire a lifelong love of numbers and a deep respect for nature.

Learning Through Play on the Shore

Discover the magic of shapes while enjoying the great outdoors! Drawing in the sand is a wonderful way to explore early geometry, spark creativity and connect with nature. Let your imagination run wild as you transform simple shapes into fun designs like sea creatures or whimsical patterns.

You'll Need to Collect:

~ A long, straight piece of driftwood (*Tip: Look for a sturdy stick that's already washed ashore. No need to break off new branches. Take only a little and never what's rare or protected. Love our Earth as you would your own family. Leave her as beautiful as you found her, honouring the interconnection we all share.*)

Now Create:

~ Start with Simple Shapes:

~ Use your driftwood stick to draw a circle, then a square, rectangle and triangle in the sand.

~ Take time to notice how each shape looks and feels different as you draw.

~ Expand Your Creations:

~ Turn your shapes into something fun: a circle could become the face of a sea monster, a triangle might be the fin of a shark and a rectangle could turn into a treasure chest.

~ Experiment with combinations to create patterns or stories in the sand.

Extend the Fun:

~ Trace and Decorate: Once you've drawn your shapes, decorate them with shells, leaves or stones.

~ Play Guess the Shape: Have someone draw a shape and guess what it is before they finish.

~ Shape Hunt: Look around and spot natural objects that match the shapes you've drawn.

Learning Made Magical:

~ This activity blends early geometry with creativity, offering endless possibilities for play and exploration. Shapes in the Sand are more than just drawings. They're connections to the natural world and the joy of discovery.

Nature's Canvas for Your Creativity

Turn ordinary shells into vibrant treasures with this simple yet delightful activity. By combining the beauty of nature with your artistic flair, you'll create colourful keepsakes that reflect your unique style. As always, collect with care. Tread lightly.

You'll Need to Collect:

- Shells (*Tip: Look for smooth, flat shells that are easy to decorate. Take only a little and never what's rare or protected. Love our Earth as you would your own family. Leave her as beautiful as you found her, honouring the interconnection we all share.*)
- Sharpie pens in a variety of colours. Choose non-toxic markers to ensure safety for the environment.

Now Create:

- Choose Your Shells: Select a few shells that inspire you with their shapes and textures.
- Decorate with Patterns: Use Sharpie pens to draw vibrant patterns on the shells.
- Try stripes, dots, swirls or geometric designs.
- Mix and match colours to make your creations pop.
- Let Your Imagination Shine: Each shell can tell its own story. Maybe it's inspired by the waves, the stars or your favourite animal.

Extend the Fun:

- Make It Personal: Write your initials or a short message on the shells.
- Create a Collection: Decorate a series of shells with complementary designs and display them together.
- Share the Joy: Gift your decorated shells to friends and family as a thoughtful keepsake.

Your Art, Your Connection:

Patterns on Shells is more than a craft. It's a way to connect with the ocean, celebrate its beauty and share your creativity with the world. Let your patterned shells serve as a reminder of your time by the sea and your commitment to protecting its treasures.

Crafting the Alphabet with Nature

Discover the magic of letters and sounds by creating the alphabet with natural materials. This tactile and creative activity blends early literacy with a connection to the natural world, making learning engaging and fun. As always, collect responsibly. Take only what you need and leave nature as beautiful as you found it.

You'll Need to Collect:

〰 Short, straight sticks of driftwood *(**Tip:** Take only a little and never what's rare or protected. Love our Earth as you would your own family. Leave her as beautiful as you found her, honouring the interconnection we all share.)*

Now Create:

〰 Form the Letters:
- Arrange the driftwood sticks on a flat surface to form each letter of the alphabet.
- Start with simple letters like A, T, or L, then move on to more complex shapes like B, R, or Q.

〰 Capture Your Work:
- Photograph each letter as you create it, ensuring the images are clear and well-lit.

〰 Complete the Alphabet:
- Rearrange the sticks as needed to create all 26 letters, one at a time.

〰 Make Alphabet Cards:
- Print the photographed letters onto individual cards, one letter per card.
- For added creativity, decorate the cards with a soft, sandy background or ocean-themed designs.

Extend the Fun:

〰 Play Games:
- Print two sets of the cards to play MEMORY, SNAP or FISH with friends and family.

〰 Practice Letter Sounds:
- Use the cards to explore letter sounds, building early phonics skills in a hands-on way.

〰 Create Words:
- Arrange the cards to spell simple words like CAT or SUN, encouraging early spelling practice.

Learning That Sticks:

By creating the alphabet with driftwood, children can experience the shapes and sounds of letters in a natural, playful way. This activity fosters a love of learning while nurturing a connection to the beauty of the natural world.

Revisit Beach Memories with Creativity

Turn your favourite holiday drawings or photos into playful paper dolls that bring your beach memories to life. This interactive craft is a delightful way to reflect on joyful experiences while creating keepsakes to treasure.

You'll Need to Collect:

- Tiny sticks *(**Tip:** Let them remind you of coconut palms swaying in the breeze. Take only a little and never what's rare or protected. Love our Earth as you would your own family. Leave her as beautiful as you found her, honouring the interconnection we all share.)*

- Sand.

- A series of happy holiday drawings or photos taken at the beach.

- Repurpose an old shadow box-style photo frame.

Now Create:

- Sprinkle sand across the base of the frame to form a miniature beach.

- Arrange the tiny sticks inside the frame, standing upright to mimic coconut tree trunks.

- Cut Out the Figures:

  - Carefully cut out the people, pets or special items from each drawing or photo, leaving a long tab to fold back.

  - Fold back the tabs to help the paper dolls stand independently.

Set the Scene:

- Position the photo dolls in the scene, arranging them to interact with the "beach" and "trees."
- Adjust and add any finishing touches until the scene feels just right.

Recount Your Memories:

- Use the paper dolls to retell your favourite beach stories.

Ask questions like:

- "Who was there?"
- "What did you see?"
- "What did you do?"
- "How did you feel?"

Extend the Fun:

Make It Interactive:

- Create additional props for your dolls, like tiny beach towels, surfboards or shells.

Swap Stories:

- Share your paper doll set with friends and invite them to recount their own beach adventures.

Keep Adding:

Each beach trip can inspire a new set of dolls, creating a growing collection of happy memories.

A Keepsake of Joyful Days:

The Big Recount transforms holiday drawings and photos into cherished storytelling tools, blending creativity, reflection and play. Let your paper dolls remind you of sunny days and the special people and places that make your beach memories so magical.

A Valentine's Gift with Heart and Nature

Celebrate Valentine's Day by creating a heartfelt, nature-inspired token for your furry friend. This simple and creative gesture is a beautiful way to express your love while embracing the natural world.

You'll Need to Collect:

- A shell with a natural hole or alternatively a responsible adult can drill a small hole (**Tip:** *Take only a little and never what's rare or protected. Love our Earth as you would your own family. Leave her as beautiful as you found her, honouring the interconnection we all share.)*
- A red Sharpie
- A long piece of sustainable string such as jute twine or bamboo cord.

Now Create:

- Prepare Your Shell:
  - Clean the shell with seawater and let it dry in the sun.
  - Use the red Sharpie to draw a heart on the shell, adding any extra designs and initials, or leave it plain if you'd like.
- Attach the Shell:
  - Thread the sustainable string or O-ring through the shell's hole.
  - Secure it to your pet's collar so they can proudly wear their Valentine's gift.
- Sing the Valentine's Song:
  - To the tune of Happy Birthday, serenade your pet with this special song:

    "Happy Valentine's to you,

    Happy Valentine's to you,

    Happy Valentine's my darling,

    Happy Valentine's to YOU."

Extend the Fun:

🌊 Capture the Moment: Take a photo of your pet wearing their Valentine shell.

🌊 Make It a Tradition: Create a new Valentine shell each year, turning it into a cherished tradition.

A Token of Love and Care:

🌊 This Be my Valentine isn't just a gift. It's a reminder of the love and connection we share with our pets and the natural world. Let it inspire kindness this Valentine's Day.

A Love Heart

Share Love Through Nature's Art

Express your love with a heart made from the treasures of the sea. This simple and heartfelt activity combines creativity with a deep connection to nature, making it a meaningful way to show someone you care.

You'll Need to Collect:

- Small shells *(**Tip:** Take only a little and never what's rare or protected. Love our Earth as you would your own family. Leave her as beautiful as you found her, honouring the interconnection we all share.)*

Now Create:

- Shape Your Heart:
  - Find a flat surface, like sand or a table, and carefully arrange the small shells into a heart shape.
  - Adjust and rearrange until your heart feels just right.
- Capture the Moment:
  - Take photos of your shell heart, experimenting with angles and lighting to make it look beautiful.
- Create Love Letters:
  - Print the photos onto blank cards or paper.
  - Write heartfelt messages to your loved ones inside, inspired by your shell creation.
- Share the Love:
  - Send your love letters to friends and family or keep them as cherished mementos.

Extend the Fun:

- Gift Your Heart: After taking photos, leave your shell heart in a special spot on the beach for others to discover.
- Make It Personal: Add initials or a meaningful word inside the heart to make it unique.
- Start a Tradition: Create a new shell heart every year as a lasting expression of love.

A Simple Act of Love:

This Love Heart activity is more than just an activity. It's a way to connect with nature and the people you cherish.

The Christmas Star

Shine Bright with a Nature-Inspired Christmas Craft

Bring the magic of the season into your home with a beautiful, handmade star made from natural materials. Combining driftwood and twinkling lights, this festive decoration celebrates creativity, sustainability and the joy of Christmas.

You'll Need to Collect:

- 5 straight pieces of driftwood, similar in length *(**Tip:** Take only a little and never what's rare or protected. Love our Earth as you would your own family. Leave her as beautiful as you found her, honouring the interconnection we all share.)*
- A long piece of sustainable string such as jute twine or bamboo cord.
- Battery-operated fairy lights

Now Create:

- Form the Star Shape:
  - Arrange the 5 pieces of driftwood into a star shape, overlapping the ends where necessary.
  - Adjust the angles until the star looks balanced and symmetrical.
- Secure the Points:
  - Use the sustainable string to tie and secure the ends of the driftwood at each point of the star. Make sure the structure is stable.
- Add the Lights:
  - Wrap the fairy lights around the star, weaving them between the driftwood pieces.
  - Use additional string to secure the lights if needed.
- Display Your Star:
  - Hang your Christmas Star on a wall, in a window or place it as a centerpiece to bring festive cheer to your space.

Extend the Fun:

- Customise Your Star: Add small decorations like shells, pinecones, or red ribbons for an extra festive touch.
- Make It Glow Outdoors: Use weatherproof fairy lights to display your star in your garden or on your front porch.

A Star with Heart:

The Christmas Star is more than just a decoration. It's a symbol of the season's magic and a reminder to celebrate with care for the Earth. Let it shine brightly, spreading warmth, joy and the beauty of nature this Christmas.

Join the Mission: Volunteer in Australia

Australia needs heroes like you! If you live near a turtle habitat, consider volunteering at a Turtle Rehabilitation Centre, where injured and sick turtles are cared for and given a second chance at life.

Did you know? The Great Barrier Reef is home to six of the world's seven species of marine turtles, but these majestic creatures are under threat - especially from plastic pollution.

Here's the heartbreaking connection: A floating plastic bag in the ocean can resemble a jellyfish, one of a turtle's favourite foods. Over time, the bag collects algae, creating a smell that turtles find irresistible. When they swallow the bag, it gets stuck in their backward-facing throats, which are designed to keep food moving down—not up. Unlike humans, turtles cannot cough the bag out, so it remains trapped in the stomach, undigested. This eventually causes the turtle to float, unable to dive for food, leading to starvation and death.

When turtles exhibit strange behaviour, alert fishermen often contact Turtle Rehabilitation Centres, who rescue and care for these struggling creatures.

This tragic plight is why your help matters. By volunteering, you can make a direct difference in the lives of these incredible animals who have swum in the ocean for millions of years.

A personal note of gratitude. To the wonderful volunteers at Cairns Turtle Rehabilitation Centre on Fitzroy Island: You are my heroes. Your dedication to rescuing and rehabilitating these beautiful creatures inspires us to take action and protect our planet.

Together, we can protect our planet. Start small, dream big and be the change.

How to Be a Planet Protector

Save the Ocean: Say no to Plastic

Our oceans need you. Plastic pollution harms marine life and our planet. It's time to make smarter choices every day.

The 7 R's of Sustainability

Before you buy, pause and ask:

- Rethink – Do I really need this?
- Refuse – Say no to single-use plastics.
- Reduce – Buy less. Choose better.
- Repurpose – Get creative and upcycle.
- Reuse – Give items a second (or third!) life.
- Recycle – Learn how to recycle properly.
- Remove – Pick up rubbish when you see it.

Every small action adds up. Start at the beach! If you spot rubbish, grab it and bin it. Ask a grown-up to help, and know that every piece you collect saves marine life and keeps the ocean clean. There's #NOPLANETB.

The Pledge

Let's make a promise to protect and love our planet. By becoming an Earth Steward, you'll help care for our beautiful world every single day.

Your Pledge

I promise to do my best,

To care for Earth,

To love and protect her,

And to always be an Earth Steward.

This is my promise and I will keep it.

Together, our small actions can create big changes.

Taking Time to Reflect: A Moment for You

In the hustle of everyday life, how often do we pause to truly reflect? The reflections in this book are invitations. Not to rush, but to linger. Each one is a gentle nudge to ponder deeply, to connect with nature and to reconnect with yourself.

Why take the time? Because reflection is where meaning takes root. It's in these quiet moments that you'll uncover insights about your interconnection to our Earth, the people around you, and the stories you carry. Each reflection is like a pebble dropped into water. It's ripples reaching far beyond the surface, sparking curiosity, wonder and sometimes even change.

Take the time to sit with each reflection. Ponder how it speaks to you and your journey. Let it settle into your heart and inspire how you engage with the world around you. These moments of stillness are a gift. One that connects to something bigger and leaves you with a renewed sense of purpose and care for our shared home.

Reflection isn't just thinking; it's feeling, imagining and dreaming. So take your time, because these reflections are not just words - they're pathways to discovery.

The Ocean as a Teacher

The ocean teaches us about the rhythms of life. How every wave returns to the shore, how the tides ebb and flow. By listening to these lessons, we can learn to live in harmony with the world around us, respecting the delicate balance that sustains all life.

The Role of Wonder and Curiosity

Never lose your sense of wonder. The ocean is full of mysteries, from the smallest creatures that dance in the shallows to the vast, unexplored depths. Let your curiosity guide you, for it is through wonder that we find the motivation to protect and preserve the beauty that surrounds us.

Intergenerational Responsibility

The ocean has been here long before any of us and it will be here long after. The care of our Earth is a responsibility we pass from one generation to the next. By nurturing a love for nature in our children, we ensure that the future stewards of this planet are equipped with the wisdom and compassion needed to protect it.

A Call to Action

Every choice you make, no matter how small, ripples through the world like a wave. Choose kindness, choose care and choose to protect our Earth. The ocean is calling and it is up to each of us to answer.

A Dedication to Future Generations

This book is dedicated to the children who will inherit our Earth. May you grow with the knowledge that you are part of something greater and may you always feel the pull of the tides, reminding you of the deep connection you share with the world around you.

Taking Time to Answer: A Journey Within

The questions in this book are more than prompts. They're doorways to discovery. They invite you to pause, think deeply and reconnect with the moments that have shaped your love for nature and the choices you make each day.

Why take the time? Because answering these questions is an act of mindfulness. It's an opportunity to reflect on your memories, your values and the role you play in protecting the world we share. Each answer is a story waiting to unfold. A chance to relive the joy of your childhood adventures, embrace the wisdom that our Earth has to offer and discover meaningful ways to give back to the world around you.

Don't rush. Sit with each question as you would with an old friend. Let the answers flow naturally, whether they come as vivid memories, quiet realisations or heartfelt promises for the future. These questions are here to spark interconnection with yourself, your loved ones and the planet.

Answering isn't just about words. It's about intention. It's about remembering what truly matters and finding new ways to honour and cherish the natural world. Take your time and let these questions guide you on a journey of reflection and purpose.

What is your favourite memory of playing in nature?

- Was it climbing trees, feeling the rough bark under your hands and the wind on your face?

- Perhaps it was running barefoot on the beach, chasing waves or collecting shells.

- Did you camp under the stars, build a cubby in the bush, make mud pies in the backyard or explore rainforest tracks with a curious heart?

- How did it feel to be completely immersed in the sights, sounds and smells of the natural world?

- Reflect on how these moments made you feel - free, joyful and connected to something bigger.

What small steps can you take to protect our Earth today?

- Could you pick up rubbish on your next walk, leaving the beach or park cleaner than you found it?

- How about choosing sustainable materials, like jute string or bamboo cord for your next project?

- Can you reduce plastic use in your home, swapping out single-use items for reusable ones?

- What about planting a tree or starting a small garden to create a habitat for wildlife?

- Share these actions with friends and family, spreading a culture of care and sustainability.

The only screen I need is sunscreen

Alison Fitzsimmons

Nature is always on my mind

Alison Fitzsimmons

My happy place is nature

Alison Fitzsimmons

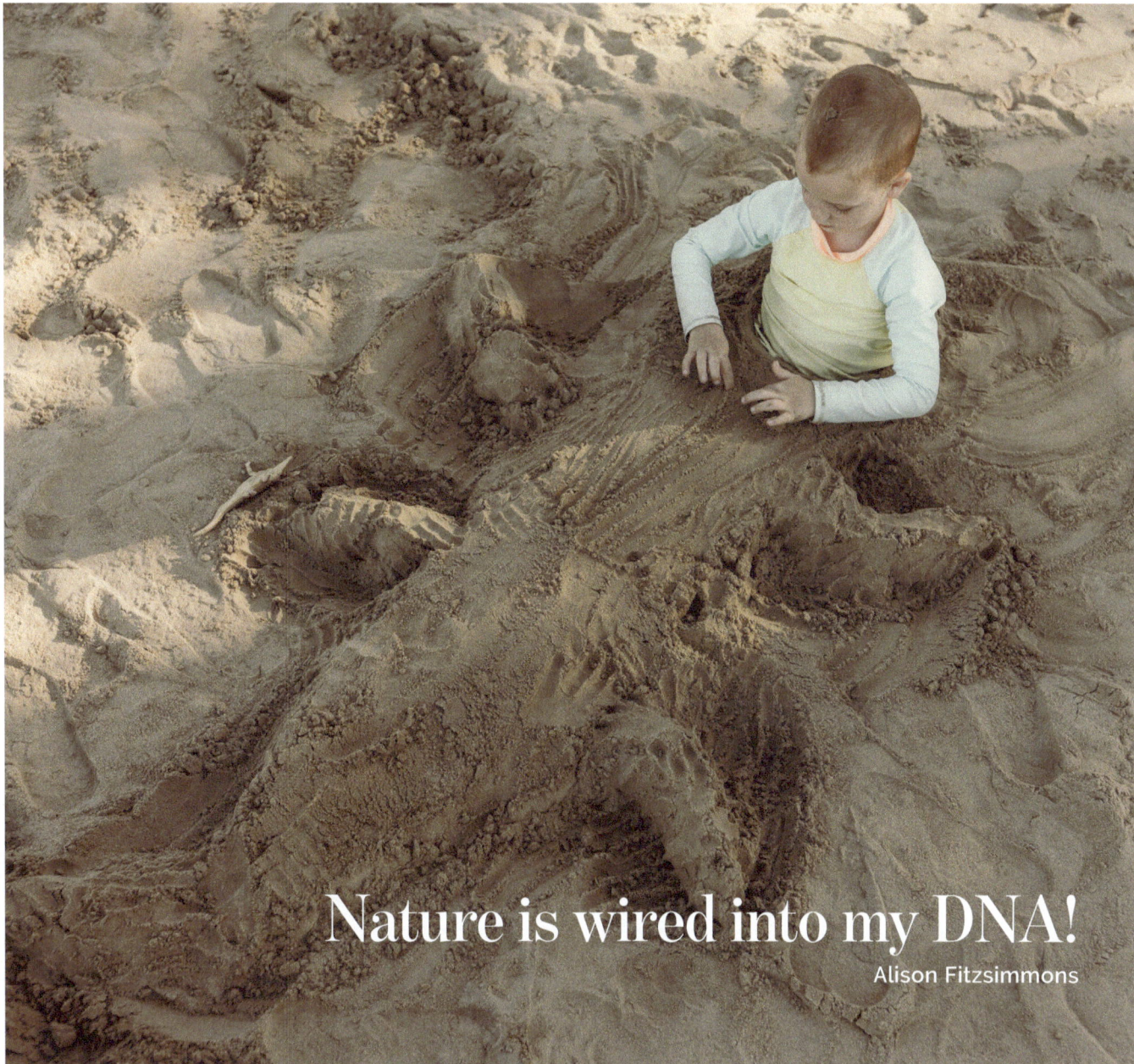

Nature is wired into my DNA!

Alison Fitzsimmons

I'm swapping screen time for nature time

Alison Fitzsimmons

The children have the last word

Alison Fitzsimmons

In the End

It is the children who bring us back to the heart of life's simple joys and timeless truths. Their laughter carries the rhythm of our Earth, their curiosity mirrors the wonder of nature and their creativity reminds us of the boundless possibilities all around us.

Through their innocent yet wise eyes, we are inspired to see the world as it is: beautiful, fragile and worth protecting. They remind us that stewardship isn't just a duty but a privilege, a promise to care for this planet so it remains a sanctuary for them and for those who come after.

In their small hands and big dreams, we see the future. And in their hearts, we rediscover the essence of what it means to love, to nurture and to belong to this shared home, we call our Earth.

Gratitude

In Gratitude to our Earth

To the gentle waves that whispered their secrets, the soft sand that held our imaginations and the driftwood, shells and sunlight that sparked our wonder - thank you, Earth, for our gifts.

You give us more than we could ever repay - joy in the smallest treasures, peace in the vastness of your oceans and moments of magic that stay with us forever.

We honour you with our care, our respect and our promise to protect your beauty - for today, for tomorrow and for all who walk these beaches after us.

Thank You

This nature play book was penned on the sacred lands of the Gimuy Walubara Yidinji people. I am deeply grateful to the traditional custodians of this ancient place for their enduring care of Country, its land, its waters, its sky, through profound knowledge, reverence and guardianship. Their ancient wisdom teaches us that everything is held in relationship, a truth that resonates deeply within me.

From my earliest memories, I have cherished the intergenerational wisdom passed down by my great-grandmother, grandmothers and parents. Their stories and love are woven into the very fabric of my being, steadfast within my DNA.

~ To my parents, Tom and Maureen, thank you for planting in me the kind of love that outlives even the tallest trees. You gave me roots to ground me and wings to soar.

When the world paused at the onset of the pandemic, so did our plans. Our family's much-anticipated beachside reunion was canceled as skies emptied and borders closed. Loved ones in Los Angeles remained distant, their contact confined to screens. Our Beach, a reminder of our interconnectedness, was conceived as I sat alone on the sand, gazing out to the horizon. I imagined sending love and protection across the Pacific, carried on the waves toward those I love.

Some stories linger long after childhood, tucked into memory like shells in a pocket. If you recognise Baby Bear's chair from the classic fairy tale The Three Bears, chances are you were read to as a child. It's a story that begins with a walk before breakfast, a quiet ritual of belonging. In my reimagining, the bears leave the woods and settle by the sea. Each morning, they enjoy a new twist on porridge, overnight oats on their beach walk.

This gentle shift inspired babybearschair.com.au, my little adventure connecting young children with stories and nature. Just as Our Beach was born from a longing for reconnection, Baby Bear's Chair reminds us that even something as simple as a walk before breakfast can help us fall in love with our Earth again. And what we love, we will protect.

~ To Crystal, thank you for holding this book like it mattered, for seeing its soul and guiding it into the world of self publishing with steady hands and a kind heart. You have been more than a publisher. You have been a midwife to something deeply loved.

~ To Kellie, you arrived with calm clarity, editing with grace and the kind of care only someone who understands the weight of words can bring. You didn't just edit - you accompanied.

~ To Astie and Kyrah, your graphic artwork sings. Every page shimmers because of you both. You did not just design. You breathed life into these words and gave them their wings.

~ To Emm, your lens does not just capture images. It listens. It watches for soul. And somehow, every click of your camera found the heartbeat of this project.

~ To Tricia, thank you for being there, unexpectedly and perfectly. You arrived like a bonus chapter. Full of grace, full of heart.

~ To Brother Jenkins Café, thank you for being my sanctuary. Most Fridays, I sat amidst the gentle hum of my tribe. Young mothers nursing babies, friends laughing over coffee, stories shared in conversation. You gave my ideas a place to land. Particularly to the senior yoga ladies whose profound joy in each other and their love of cake, inspired my search for my weavers.

- To Julie and Calvine, thank you for weaving more than string bags. You wove story, memory and meaning into every loop and knot. What you have created will outlast trends. It is heirloom work and I see you in every strand.

- To Margie and Sally, thank you for walking the integral ecology path ahead of me and inviting me to follow. You have helped me see how the cosmos lives inside every shell, every sigh of wind, every child's curiosity.

- To Pope Francis, thank you for the gift of Laudato Si', a song of love for our common home. Your words echo through every page of this book and every beat of my heart. They have shaped my way of seeing, listening and living.

- To my earliest supporters, Colleen, Karen, Julie, Coral, Madonna, Sandy, Gail, Toni and Elizabeth, thank you for holding these pages when they were still tender and new. Your encouragement, thoughtful words and quiet belief helped this book find its voice.

- To Fran, my oldest friend, my first kindergarten companion and my steadfast collaborator. How I have loved Fridays filled with cheering the other on as we work on our projects. Your unwavering support and shared enthusiasm have been instrumental to me. Thank you for being a constant source of inspiration and joy throughout this journey.

- To the children, Marney, Lily, Oscar, and Seffy, thank you for playing with wonder wide open. You reminded me what it means to belong to this Earth, to love it like a playground, a mother, a secret world full of magic.

- To the children's parents, Tammi and Robin, Emm and Benji, thank you for growing children who know how to listen to the wind and dance in tide pools. You are raising the ones who will heal the world.

- To Pearl, my salt kissed, sea loving, loyal girl, you have been my reminder to run wild, sleep deeply and always come back to the sea.

- To my family and friends, thank you for holding space for this work, for cheering from the sidelines, and for reminding me that creation is always a shared act.

- To my three little sisters, Jill, Hayley and Melanie each of you is a vibrant thread in the tapestry of my life. Your laughter, wisdom and unwavering support remind me of the strength found in sisterhood. Thank you for being my cheerleaders and forever friends.

- To my children, Harriette and Max, and to their partners, Ross and Jemma, thank you for being the joy I carry in every breath. You have taught me everything worth knowing about love.

- To the love of my life, Terry, thank you for loving me through every tide and season. You are woven into my heart.

- If you have picked up this book, thank you. It means you believe, as I do, that nature is sacred, children are treasures and that somewhere between the sand and the sea, we remember who we truly are. Kin.

A Special Message to my Granddaughter

Hola Claudia

To my granddaughter, Claudia, this is for you. May you grow with love for our Earth, finding wonder in every moment. You are our light and everything I do is for your future.

You are my little heart's arrow.

With Love,
Nana xoxo

A word from the Author

Dear Friend,

This book is a piece of my heart and a story of interconnection; personal and universal.

I was born at Machans Beach, a small coastal community just north of Cairns in Far North Queensland, Australia. The photographs in this book were taken where the Barron River meets the Coral Sea, at Redden Island. To reach this magical spot, you simply follow Cinderella Street and cross a little bridge, a pathway to beauty and memory.

The photographer is my cousin, a young mother, capturing the joy of her children and their cousin playing by the sea. Her own mother, my first cousin and childhood playmate, flew in from Sydney to surprise me that day. Three generations of mothers, daughters, grandmothers and grandchildren gathered, bound by place, family, and love. On that day, my own daughter felt a quiet excitement, suspecting she was pregnant. She was.

This personal story mirrors the ocean's story. The ocean is life. Without it, there is no rain, no rivers, no forests, no us.

But we've taken so much and given so little back. The ocean needs us: our care, our protection, our love.

This book is a call to action and a reminder: the ocean isn't just a place to visit; it's a part of who we are. Let's teach the next generation to cherish it, just as we cherish each other.

Thank you for sharing this journey with me.

With hope,
Alison Fitzsimmons
xoxo

Index

A   Activity: 24, 27, 28, 30, 35, 36, 41, 42, 44, 48, 50, 52, 54, 55, 57, 62, 64, 65, 66, 68, 69, 75

B   Beauty: 3, 13, 18, 21, 27, 29, 30, 33, 35, 36, 39, 41, 42, 46, 48, 57, 58, 59, 61, 62, 66, 69, 77, 85, 96, 102, 106

C   Creativity: 6, 13, 18, 24, 28, 29, 35, 41, 42, 48, 51, 52, 53, 54, 56, 57, 58, 62, 65, 66, 69, 70, 71, 75, 76, 94

       Connection: 5, 13, 21, 28, 31, 36, 45, 47, 53, 54, 57, 59, 65, 66, 68, 69, 73, 75, 80, 85

D   Discovery: 17, 41, 65, 84, 86

E   Explore: 13, 21, 24, 41, 42, 56, 62, 65, 69, 87

F   Family: 14, 24, 27, 29, 30, 33, 36, 41, 42, 44, 46, 47, 50, 52, 53, 54, 57, 58, 62, 65, 66, 69, 70, 72, 75, 77, 87, 102

G   Gratitude: 32, 33, 80, 96

       Generations: 14, 61, 85, 102

J   Joy: 14, 17, 18, 21, 29, 35, 41, 50, 51, 52, 53, 54, 65, 66, 76, 77, 86, 96, 102

K   Kindness: 73, 85

M   Mandalas: 32, 33

N   Nature: 5, 6, 13, 18, 21, 22, 24, 30, 32, 33, 35, 36, 41, 42, 46, 48, 50, 51, 52, 53, 54, 56, 57, 58, 61, 62, 65, 66, 68, 72, 76, 77, 84, 86, 87, 89, 90, 91, 92, 94, 106

O   Ocean: 2, 3, 6, 10, 27, 30, 31, 44, 45, 46, 47, 54, 66, 69, 80, 82, 85, 96, 102

P   Patterns: 32, 33, 41, 48, 56, 57, 59, 65, 66

R   Reflection: 31, 59, 71, 84, 86

       Rhythm: 3, 10, 44, 94, 107

S   Stewardship: 18, 94

V   Valentine: 72, 73

W   Wonder: 3, 5, 6, 13, 14, 18, 25, 31, 41, 42, 59, 84, 85, 94, 97, 101, 106, 107

       Weaving: 21, 56, 57, 77

Why This Back Cover Image Matters

This image holds the heart of Our Beach. Two children, cousins, lie on their tummies in the sand, gently colouring the surfaces of small shells with bright strokes of wonder. They are not performing. They are simply present. Immersed in a moment of quiet concentration, side by side, held by our Earth. I chose this image because it tells the story of what matters most: children in relationship with nature, with each other and with their own sense of awe. It is not posed. It is sacred. It reminds us that with time, space and love, children will always find their way back to the wild beauty of the world. And if we are lucky, they will take us with them.

About Alison Fitzsimmons

Alison Fitzsimmons is a writer, educator and new grandmother who believes that childhood is not a race, but a rhythm. She lives with her husband and their dogs in a house with 43 steps, tucked in the rainforest of Far North Queensland. Our Beach is her love letter to Earth, to wonder and to the small hands that remind us how to pay attention.

Follow Alison on Instagram & Facebook:
@babybearschair.com.au

Free Educator Notes Available Online
Includes links to the EYLF v2.0, Australian Curriculum, Montessori and Reggio approaches.
Perfect for classrooms, home learning and therapy settings.

Scan the QR code to explore and download.

From the Publisher

Our Beach is a gentle, heartfelt invitation to rediscover the natural world through the fresh and curious eyes of a child. Alison masterfully captures the magic of beachcombing and the ocean's timeless rhythms, weaving a narrative that feels both intimate and universal.

This beautifully crafted book goes beyond observation; it invites readers of all ages to engage actively with nature through creative, eco-friendly activities. From crafting keepsakes with treasures found along the shore to thoughtful reflections on environmental stewardship, Our Beach nurtures a deep sense of connection and responsibility toward the planet.

Congratulations Alison, on this soulful journey that invites us to reconnect, reflect, and celebrate the beauty and wisdom of the natural world. It has been an absolute pleasure to help you bring *Our Beach* to life.

Crystal Leonardi
Bowerbird Publishing
www.crystalleonardi.com

www.ingramcontent.com/pod-product-compliance
Lightning Source LLC
Chambersburg PA
CBHW041240020426
42333CB00002B/24